THE ELEVENTH DOCTOR:
MATT SMITH

BBC Children's Books
Published by the Penguin Group
Penguin Books Ltd, 80 Strand, London, WC2R ORL, England
Penguin Group (USA) Inc., 375 Hudson Street, New York 10014, USA
Penguin Books (Australia) Ltd, 250 Camberwell Road, Camberwell, Victoria 3124, Australia
(A division of Pearson Australia Group PTY Ltd)
Canada, India, New Zealand, South Africa
Published by BBC Children's Books, 2010
Text and design © Children's Character Books
Written by Oli Smith
With thanks to Matt Smith

Picture Credits:
Benedict Cumberbatch page 10 © Jonathan Hordle/Rex Features
James Nesbitt page 10 © Rex Features
Robert Carlyle page 11 © Jonathan Hordle/Rex Features
Paterson Joseph page 11 © ITV/Rex Features
Joanna Lumley page 11 © Geoffrey Swaine/Rex Features
David Walliams page 11 © David Fisher/Rex Features
Matt Smith and Karen Gillan page 31 © Rex Features
Albert Einstein page 43 Phtotographer: Arthur Sasse © Bettmann/CORBIS
Richard Curtis page 43 © Crollalanza/Rex Features
Matt Smith pages 48-49 © Beretta/Sims/Rex Features
Images pages 50-51 Copyright © BBC
Matt Smith page 57 © Brian J Ritchie/Rex Features
Matt Smith page 60 © Jon Beretta/Rex Features
Matt Smith page 61 © Jonathan Hordle/Rex Features

10 9 8 7 6 5 4 3 2 1
ISBN: 978-1-40590-687-6
Printed in Italy

DOCTOR WHO

THE ELEVENTH DOCTOR: MATT SMITH

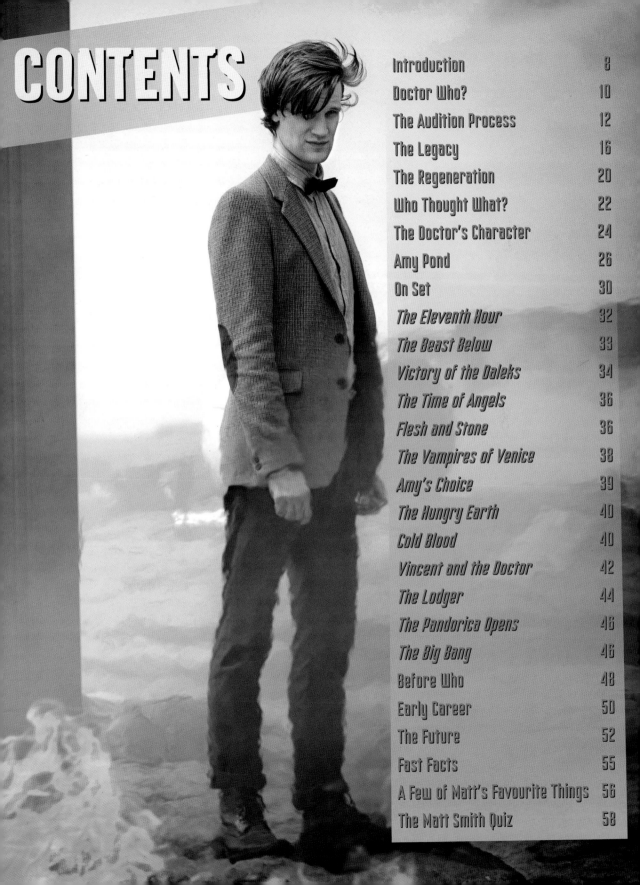

CONTENTS

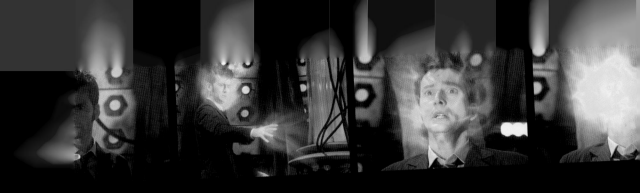

INTRODUCTION

On 3 January 2009, nearly seven million viewers crowded around their televisions for a special one-off episode of *Doctor Who Confidential*. It had been over two months since David Tennant – arguably the most popular actor ever to play the role of the Doctor – had announced that he was leaving *Doctor Who* after a series of specials at the end of the year. Since then, both the media and fans from across the world had engaged in wild and enthusiastic speculation as to who could possibly take over the lead role in science-fiction's longest running television show.

Who was going to be the Eleventh Doctor?

But when the fresh-faced young actor cast as the nation's favourite Time Lord appeared on screen enthusing about the prospect of bringing to life the latest incarnation of the Doctor with show runner Steven Moffat, TV audiences were left with more questions than answers – mostly, who on Earth was Matt Smith?

Throughout the show's forty-seven year history, the role of the Doctor has always been faced with public scrutiny. It is surprising how many of the actors who were given the role were relative unknowns before their casting – a choice that was often seen as being beneficial to the series, allowing viewers to see the character of the Doctor more easily without the barrier that a big name can bring to the role. Matt Smith,

however, took this concept to extremes. Being the youngest actor ever to take the part, his modest amount of television work and handful of critically-acclaimed theatre roles caused the public to cast doubts on whether Matt Smith was capable of handling the biggest role on British television. They needn't have worried.

The Eleventh Doctor exploded onto our screens on 3 April 2010 and Matt Smith instantly confirmed that Steven Moffat's casting decision had been perfect. With his (cool) bow tie, gangly gait and a jacket that caused sales of tweed to skyrocket, Matt Smith flavoured his Doctor with elements of the Time Lord's previous incarnations, while simultaneously giving the part something entirely his own. His Doctor is funny, childish, angry and wise — often in the same scene — and with his new companion, Amy Pond, a regenerated TARDIS, sonic screwdriver and even Daleks, the Doctor's adventures continue to be as popular as ever.

But the question remains, and throughout this book we talk to the man behind the Eleventh Doctor, about his work before *Doctor Who*, how he became an actor and his life outside the world of television. Over the following pages, he'll guide us through the birth of the Doctor's latest incarnation, from his first audition to the genesis of his outfit, right the way through to the final shots of the epic series finale and beyond.

Who is Matt Smith?

Let's find out...

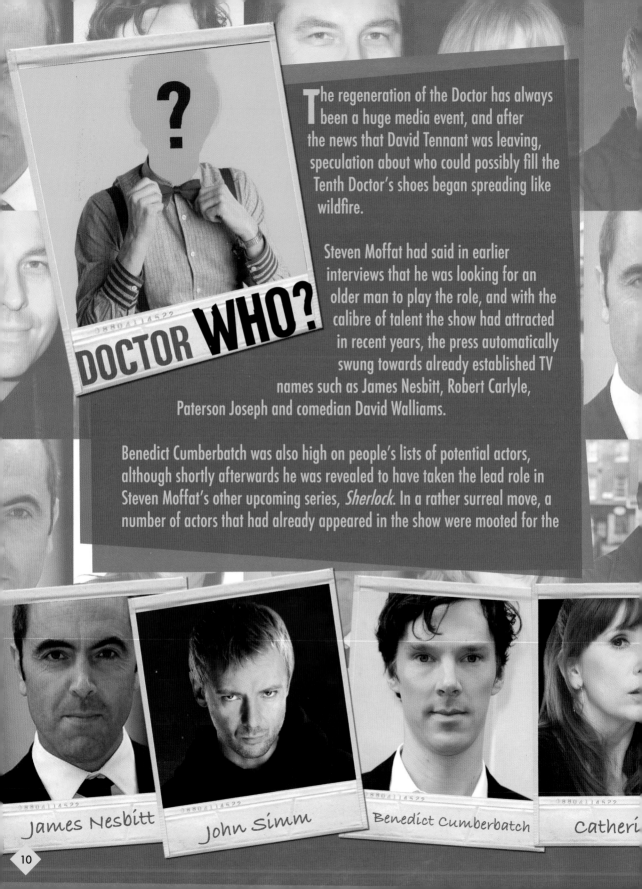

DOCTOR WHO?

The regeneration of the Doctor has always been a huge media event, and after the news that David Tennant was leaving, speculation about who could possibly fill the Tenth Doctor's shoes began spreading like wildfire.

Steven Moffat had said in earlier interviews that he was looking for an older man to play the role, and with the calibre of talent the show had attracted in recent years, the press automatically swung towards already established TV names such as James Nesbitt, Robert Carlyle, Paterson Joseph and comedian David Walliams.

Benedict Cumberbatch was also high on people's lists of potential actors, although shortly afterwards he was revealed to have taken the lead role in Steven Moffat's other upcoming series, *Sherlock*. In a rather surreal move, a number of actors that had already appeared in the show were mooted for the

James Nesbitt

John Simm

Benedict Cumberbatch

Catheri

role, including John Simm, David Morrissey, and even Catherine Tate and Billie Piper. The prospect of the Doctor becoming a woman has always been a favourite news story during the months surrounding a regeneration – and actually happened during a Children in Need sketch written by Steven Moffat in 1999, in which Joanna Lumley appeared as the Doctor's fourteenth incarnation.

By the time the announcement came, the hype surrounding the new Doctor was enormous. When Matt Smith finally set the rumour-mill to rest, he defied not only the media speculation, but also Moffat's original thoughts on what type of actor could carry the role – a testament to just how impressive he was during his audition.

Robert Carlyle

David Morrissey

Joanna Lumley

David Walliams

Billie Piper

Paterson Joseph

THE WEEK BEFORE

Barely a week before Matt's agent discovered that David Tennant was leaving the show and arranged an audition, his mother texted him suggesting that he would make a great Doctor. But his innate "Doctor-ness" had been spotted even before then, and while at university his striped scarf had earned him the nickname "Doctor Who".

AUDITIONING THE DOCTOR

The audition process was both difficult and unique. Matt was provided with a wide variety of scenes the night before – too many to learn all of them in their entirety – and he had to know his way around their basic structure before acting them out the next day. He was determined to bring something new to the role, and do his own thing with the part. The brave decisions and strange choices in his readings of the lines were what attracted Steven Moffat's attention.

> *'Matt had to keep the part a secret – even his flatmate didn't know he was going to be the Eleventh Doctor!'*

THE OTHER DOCTOR

Steven Moffat first saw Matt Smith during the auditions for his other show, *Sherlock*. Matt auditioned for the part of Doctor Watson, but whilst Steven was impressed, he considered Matt to be more of a Sherlock Holmes due to his eccentricities. Matt had already been put on the list of potential Doctors by that point, so Steven was able to get a sneaky preview before his audition for the Doctor.

KEEPING IT QUIET

During the period between his casting and the announcement, Matt had to keep the part a secret – even his flatmate didn't know he was going to be the Eleventh Doctor! Eventually, the pressure of keeping quiet meant that he had to tell *someone*, so he went to his dad, a fan of the Fourth Doctor – Tom Baker – and said, "Just call me the Doctor!" He was immensely proud of his son and offered support during Matt's early reservations about being able to play the part.

> *'...his innate "Doctor-ness" had been spotted'*

THE AUDITION PROCESS

With a shortlist of actors drawn up by the production team, the arduous process of auditioning the new Doctor began, but the team didn't have long to wait before the future Eleventh Doctor arrived. Auditioning on the first day, Matt Smith's quirky performance impressed immediately, and once the three weeks of auditions had ended, Steven Moffat and executive producer Piers Wenger declared that it had "always been Matt".

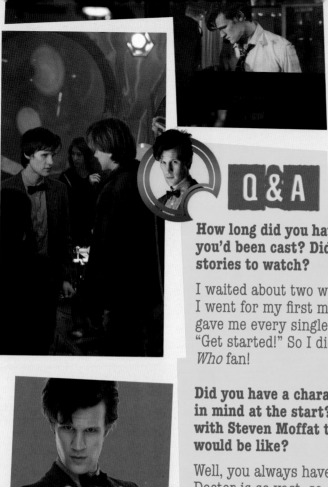

Q&A

How long did you have to wait to hear that you'd been cast? Did anyone recommend any stories to watch?

I waited about two weeks in all from the time I went for my first meeting. Afterwards, they gave me every single episode on DVD and said, "Get started!" So I did, and now I'm a huge *Who* fan!

Did you have a character for your Doctor in mind at the start? Did you work closely with Steven Moffat to establish what he would be like?

Well, you always have a blueprint, but the Doctor is so vast, so great and so complex that the more you play him, the more he surprises you. He can go anywhere and behave in any way really, and he's always the cleverest fella in the room! Steven, of course, had a huge say in who the Eleventh Doctor was, but he's also very gracious about my ideas. The Doctor's character unfolded for me, as I imagine it did for the people who watched the show.

What did you consider the character of the Doctor and the nature of the show to be like from your memories? Do you think it's important to know about past Doctors, or would you rather come to the role 'unencumbered'?

The latter, definitely – to imitate is a danger. Creatively, it's about risk, so I took risks. The Doctor's an alien, so anything goes. He gives people one chance, whether they're bad or good, but you cross him at your peril! I knew he should be funny. I knew he was a hero. But you can't play these things too broadly, as Lindsay Duncan once remarked to me, "Darling, it's all about detail." So I tried to find the detail of the man. I looked at his history; all the bloodshed he's seen and caused is important, I think, and I never really wanted him to seem moralistic or preachy. To know the history of the show is important – not only because it's so good!

THE LEGACY

BEGINNING IN NOVEMBER 1963, *DOCTOR WHO* IS THE WORLD'S LONGEST RUNNING SCIENCE FICTION TELEVISION PROGRAMME, AND ICONS SUCH AS THE DALEKS, THE TARDIS AND EVEN THE FOURTH DOCTOR'S LONG SCARF HAVE BECOME INGRAINED IN BRITISH CULTURE OVER THE DECADES. ORIGINALLY ENDING IN 1989, THE SHOW RETURNED IN 2005 UNDER THE HELM OF WRITER RUSSELL T DAVIES, WHO MADE THE SHOW MORE POPULAR THAN IT HAS EVER BEEN BEFORE. THIS SERIES A NEW PRODUCTION TEAM TOOK OVER AND WITH IT CAME A NEW DOCTOR, IN THE GUISE OF MATT SMITH, AND A NEW SHOWRUNNER – THE ACCLAIMED WRITER STEVEN MOFFAT.

THE THEME TUNE

Originally composed by Ron Grainer and arranged by Delia Derbyshire, and recently updated by series composer Murray Gold, the iconic theme tune to *Doctor Who* is often hailed as one of the best pieces of electronic music created by the BBC Radiophonic Workshop, which pioneered the genre during the sixties. Its pulsing bass line and spooky melody remain relatively unchanged to this day, and it has been covered by a variety of musicians, including the electronic dance artists Orbital.

THE DOCTOR

The Doctor is a Time Lord from the planet Gallifrey. Time Lords have a vast understanding of time travel but a policy of non-intervention in the affairs of others. Bored with the stagnant civilisation of his people, the Doctor "borrowed" a TARDIS to travel the universe in search of excitement and adventure. Over nine hundred years old, the Doctor has two hearts and, like the rest of his people, the ability to cheat death via a process known as regeneration.

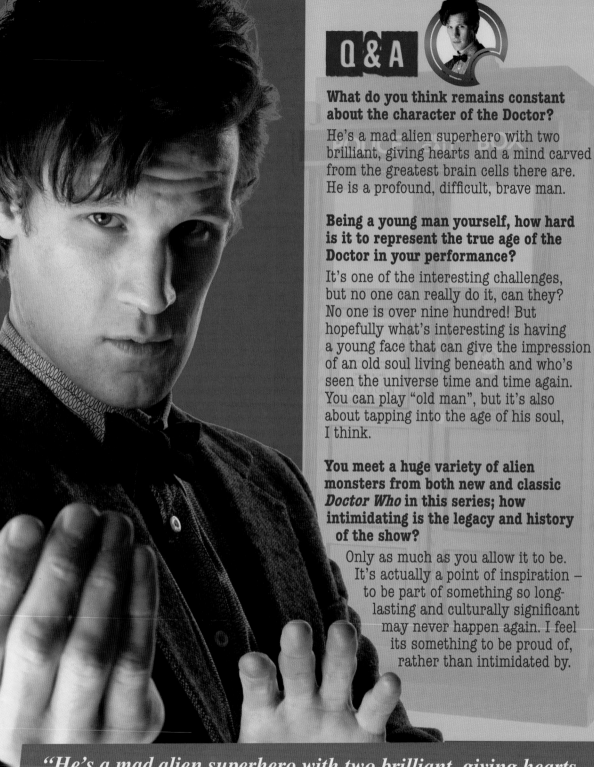

Q&A

What do you think remains constant about the character of the Doctor?

He's a mad alien superhero with two brilliant, giving hearts and a mind carved from the greatest brain cells there are. He is a profound, difficult, brave man.

Being a young man yourself, how hard is it to represent the true age of the Doctor in your performance?

It's one of the interesting challenges, but no one can really do it, can they? No one is over nine hundred! But hopefully what's interesting is having a young face that can give the impression of an old soul living beneath and who's seen the universe time and time again. You can play "old man", but it's also about tapping into the age of his soul, I think.

You meet a huge variety of alien monsters from both new and classic *Doctor Who* in this series; how intimidating is the legacy and history of the show?

Only as much as you allow it to be. It's actually a point of inspiration – to be part of something so long-lasting and culturally significant may never happen again. I feel its something to be proud of, rather than intimidated by.

"He's a mad alien superhero with two brilliant, giving hearts and a mind carved from the greatest brain cells there are."

THE FIFTH DOCTOR:
Peter Davison **1982-1984**

THE TENTH DOCTOR:
David Tennant **2005-2010**

THE FOURTH DOCTOR:
Tom Baker **1974-1981**

THE NINTH DOCTOR:
Christopher Eccleston **2005**

THE THIRD DOCTOR:
Jon Pertwee **1970-1974**

THE EIGHTH DOCTOR:
Paul McGann **1996**

THE SECOND DOCTOR:
Patrick Troughton **1966-1969**

THE SEVENTH DOCTOR:
Sylvester McCoy **1987-1996**

THE FIRST DOCTOR:
William Hartnell **1963-1966**

THE SIX DOCTOR:
Colin Baker **1984-1986**

PREVIOUS DOCTORS

THE REGENERATION

The genesis of the Eleventh Doctor was a complex procedure. Filmed amongst the pyrotechnics of an exploding TARDIS, the production team's official handover took place at the precise moment of the regeneration, with Russell T Davies and Julie Gardner on set for David Tennant's final lines before leaving to make room for Steven Moffat (who had written Matt's first) and Piers Wenger to oversee Matt's arrival. Russell's first meeting with the new Doctor occurred when the two of them bumped into each other during Matt's walk to set, and both David and Matt posed for a series of publicity pictures as the crew prepared to resume filming.

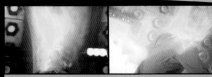

REGENERATION

The process of regeneration takes place when a Time Lord has suffered a fatal injury. Every cell in their body dies to be replaced with a new configuration – literally a new man – and the process often emits a huge amount of energy, sometimes pouring out of the body in a stream of light or, in the case of the Fourth Doctor, rippling backwards through his own timeline. Originally termed a "renewal" upon its first occurrence, the term "regeneration" was not coined until the arrival of the Fourth Doctor.

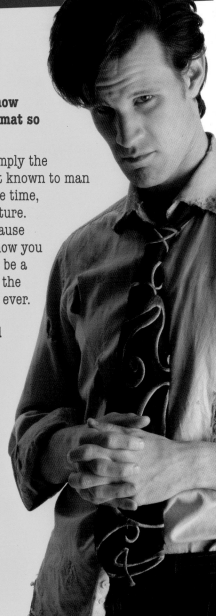

The Doctor has regenerated a total of ten times throughout his life:

THE FIRST REGENERATION: The First Doctor's old body was simply worn out when he collapsed on the floor of the TARDIS after his first encounter with the Cybermen and transformed into the Second Doctor.

THE SECOND REGENERATION: Put on trial by his own people for interference in the affairs of others, the Second Doctor was found guilty and forced to regenerate as he began an exile on Earth.

THE THIRD REGENERATION: After absorbing a massive dose of radiation on the planet Metebelis Three, during a battle with a huge spider-queen, the Third Doctor got lost in the Time Vortex, before finally returning to UNIT HQ on Earth to regenerate into the Fourth Doctor.

THE FOURTH REGENERATION: Whilst saving the universe from being held to ransom by a rival Time Lord known as the Master, the Fourth Doctor fell from the gantry of a radio tower, merging with the ghost of his future self to become the Fifth Doctor.

THE FIFTH REGENERATION: After becoming infected with a deadly disease on the planet Androzani Minor, the Fifth Doctor sacrificed his life by giving the only cure to his companion Peri.

THE SIXTH REGENERATION: The circumstances surrounding the regeneration of the Sixth Doctor are vague, but it is assumed that he was fatally injured during the Rani's attack on the TARDIS, resulting in the arrival of the Seventh Doctor.

THE SEVENTH REGENERATION: Transporting the Master's remains back to Gallifrey, the TARDIS crash-landed on Earth, with the Seventh Doctor stepping out into the middle of a gang shoot-out in San Francisco. He died later in hospital and was resurrected in the morgue as the Eighth Doctor.

THE EIGHTH REGENERATION: The nature of the Eighth Doctor's end is unknown, and is assumed to be lost in the chaos that surrounded the Last Great Time War between the Time Lords and the Daleks.

THE NINTH REGENERATION: The Ninth Doctor sacrificed himself to save his companion, Rose, who had absorbed the Time Vortex from the heart of the TARDIS to defeat the newly resurrected Daleks.

THE TENTH REGENERATION: Like the Third Doctor, the Tenth regenerated when he received a massive dose of radiation after saving an old man named Wilf, who had become trapped during the Master's attempt to resurrect the Time Lords. The TARDIS was nearly destroyed in the process.

Q&A

What's it like being in a show that can regenerate its format so drastically?

The regeneration idea is simply the cleverest televisual concept known to man (or alien). You can move the time, technology, politics and culture. The stories are infinite because there's nothing to govern how you tell them. It's a privilege to be a part of what I believe to be the greatest television concept ever.

It took you a while to shed the last of Tennant's costume and screwdriver. Did your performance change once you got into "your" outfit?

Of course! Shoes and clothes shape the way we move and feel. The same is true of the Doctor.

WHO Thought WHAT?

Press and fans alike had plenty to say about there being a new Doctor in the TARDIS, but luckily, everyone was more than impressed with what they saw!

"By the end of the episode in his tweed jacket and bow tie, like an indie-band Professor Quatermass, all had been forgotten about his illustrious predecessor. Indeed Matt Smith might turn out to be one of the best Time Lords of the lot."

THE MAIL ON SUNDAY

"From the moment he appeared, dangling from the architrave of his time machine, the new boy demonstrated that he can more than fill the shoes of his predecessor. Matt Smith fights aliens. He wears tweed. He loves custard. He is the Doctor. And he might be more the Doctor than anyone before."

THE INDEPENDENT ON SUNDAY

"Matt Smith is a Time Lord for the Twitter generation."

THE TIMES

"Last night Matt Smith's debut as the 11th Time Lord got the thumbs-up, with fans flooding web forums to heap praise on the new star."

THE SUNDAY MIRROR

"So, the new bloke. What's he like? Is he any good? Well that's easy enough – Matt Smith is terrific. He's quirky without being irritating; he's likeable, witty and bursting with joie de vivre."

RADIO TIMES

"Matt Smith is thoroughly believable as the ancient Time Lord. As the Doctor shouted last night, "Who da man?" Despite his boyish looks, Matt most certainly is."

THE PEOPLE

"This series has got off to a brilliant start – it's taken on a whole new lease of life. The casting is fantastic, the stories are spot on – it must be a great time to be eight years old."

THE SUN

"Part preppy public-school head boy, part gung-ho adventurer and part 'nutty professor' – a boy-racer in geography-teacher elbow patches."

THE GUARDIAN

Where do you see the character of your Doctor progressing in the future and how would you say your interpretation of the Doctor has changed since you started?

Who knows where it will go? It will change I'm sure, but I need to see the scripts before I know how and where to take the character.

I think I'm more in control of the language than I was at the start of the series. I feel I know the man a little better. He feels a bit more "lived in", I suppose.

A.

B.

D.

THE DOCTOR'S

During a regeneration, the Doctor's mind is literally 'shaken up' and whilst Steven Moffat has been keen to emphasise that the Doctor is always the same man, different incarnations often tend to emphasise different personality traits during their lifetimes.

A. Braces – often chosen to match the colours of both his bow tie and shirt, the Doctor's braces were a subtle reminder to Amy Pond of his existence during the series finale.

B. Tweed Jacket – a number of costume designers on the show have been keen to emphasise that the Doctor needs a recognisable silhouette – from the Ninth Doctor's leather jacket, and the Tenth's pinstriped suit, right back to the Fourth's long coat and scarf. The tweed jacket adds an air of the 'professor' to the young man, and harks back to Indiana Jones' 'academic action man'.

C. The Bow Tie – they're cool, aren't they?

D. Boots – practical.

E. A Fez – initially Matt Smith was keen for the Doctor to wear a hat, although considering Steven Moffat's treatment of the Doctor's fez in his script, it appears that he may not be so keen!

F. Rolled-up trousers – the Doctor's long, gangly legs are awkward enough without his trousers getting in the way!

C.

F.

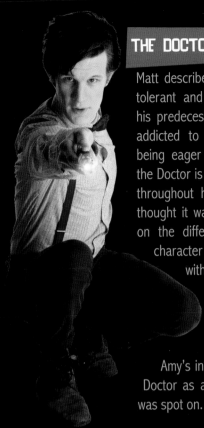

Matt describes his Doctor as less tolerant and more reckless than his predecessor, as well as being addicted to time travel. Despite being eager to demonstrate that the Doctor is always the same man throughout his regenerations, he thought it was important to focus on the different aspects of the character that come to the fore with each new incarnation. He was also eager to add some of his own personality to the role. It seems that Amy's initial description of the Doctor as a "madman in a box" was spot on.

CHARACTER

BOW TiES AND BOHEMiANS

Although both Steven and Matt were keen not to have the Doctor's costume overshadow his persona, they, along with costume designer Ray Holman, took a great deal of time experimenting with various looks to make sure it set Matt's Doctor off perfectly. Initially they experimented with a variety of coats, before almost going for a rakish pirate-explorer affair. But Matt still didn't feel comfortable, and in the end he brought in his own tweed jacket and braces. The production team were sold almost immediately, but concerns were raised when he asked to try a bow tie with the new outfit. In the end though, they all agreed that his new 'professor' style was perfect, and the bow tie became the most iconic part of his costume!

AMY POND

Throughout all his adventures through space and time, the Doctor has rarely travelled alone, and the companions that have joined him in the TARDIS have come from a myriad of different worlds and walks of life. Not only are the Doctor's adventures more fun when shared, but the presence of his best friends has been known to save his life, not only from the terrifying monsters he encounters, but from himself as well. With a new Doctor came a new companion and the media speculation surrounding her casting proved to be almost as fierce as that which followed the change of Doctor. Names such as Hannah Murray and Lily Allen were touted for the role until finally the fiery-haired Karen Gillan was revealed.

KAREN'S CAREER

Born on 22 November 1987, Karen Gillan began studying acting in Edinburgh before moving to London to finish her degree. She began work as a model while appearing as a guest character on a number of TV dramas, before finally becoming a regular cast member of the comedy sketch-series *The Kevin Bishop Show*. Her involvement with *Doctor Who* began two years before she got the part as Amy Pond as, in 2008, she was cast as a soothsayer in the Tenth Doctor story, *The Fires of Pompeii*.

PANIC MOON

Matt's first meeting with his companion-to-be, Karen Gillan, was during the later stages of the auditioning process. This was codenamed "panic moon", an anagram of "companion". He was brought in to read scenes with the final shortlist of actresses. The chemistry between the two was immediately obvious to all involved, despite Karen claiming to have been slightly intimidated at first by the prospect of acting alongside the Doctor! Matt thinks that the pair really bonded during their first day of filming as they were both newcomers to the series — a situation that rarely happens in *Doctor Who* where companions and Doctors tend to overlap.

Q & A

Why do you think Amy Pond and the Doctor work so well together?

Because they're both as mad as one another, it creates a weird alien balance!

Amy Pond has a very unique relationship with your Doctor. How did you explore that dynamic of him being her 'imaginary friend'?

Well, the Doctor is always leaving her and returning – there's a romance in that. Not literal boy-girl stuff, more of a romantic notion perhaps. I tried to realise that as brilliantly as it was written by Steven.

What is yours and Karen's relationship like on set?

I like to annoy her as much as possible – she thinks of me as her cooler, less handsome older brother! But as soon as the camera starts rolling, work becomes the main focus and we get down to the nitty gritty of making *Doctor Who*. I'm proud of Karen though, she works so hard and is really very, very funny! I'm fond of her, it must be said!

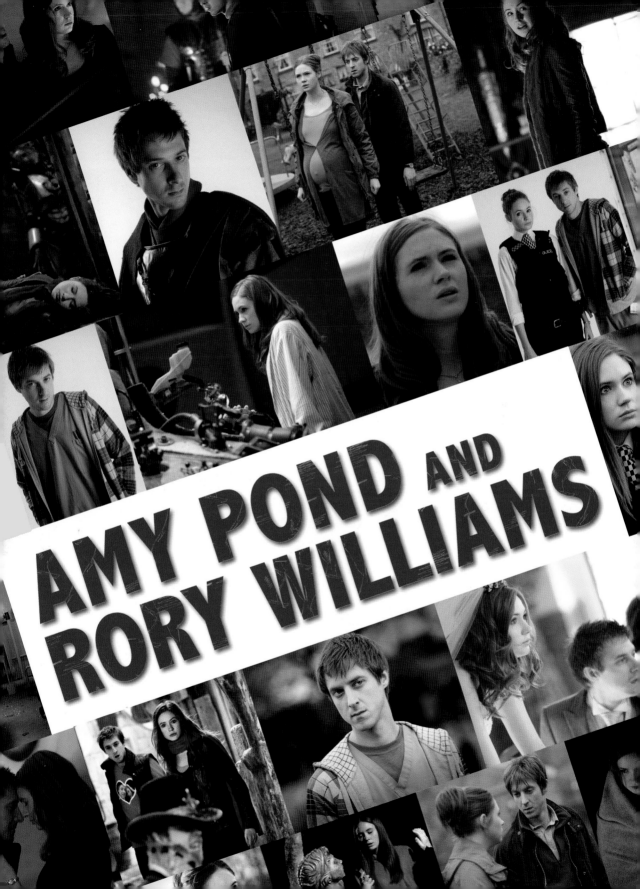

AMY POND AND RORY WILLIAMS

ON SET

Q & A

How long does it take to shoot a series and how many breaks do you get?
It takes nine months to film the series, with two weeks off at Christmas.

Because of the long hours, it can get very tiring, but does it also mean that you tend to bond with the cast and crew a lot more than on other shows?
You spend so much time together that you become this kind of work-friend-family unit. I have made some great friends up in Wales where we shoot and Karen and I have become very close as well.

What are the usual day-to-day struggles for you filming the show?

The weather! The cold, the rain, time and lines – there are so many! But we put our heads down, hold hands and battle on. Really, the challenges are the best bit – apart from the rain!

What was it like stepping onto your TARDIS for the first time?

I was like a kid in a sweet shop. I took a video camera so that I'd have a record of it forever!

Do you know what all the buttons etc are supposed to do and do any of them actually work?

Of course – they give you a manual! Each station has a purpose and I could name all the controls, right down to the button for tomato ketchup!

How does the action and special effects laden nature of the show alter your performance from more traditional forms of drama?

It takes time, of course, and requires you to use your imagination. Often the enemy looming over you is in fact a tennis ball on some string, but it's just great fun really.

THE BEGINNING

Fans' first shots of the new Doctor's costume, TARDIS and sonic screwdriver came on 20 July 2009, when filming began on Episode 4: *The Time of Angels*. This was one of the first scripts Matt had read, and with such familiar allies and monsters in the form of River Song and the Weeping Angels, it proved the perfect story in which to kick-start the Eleventh Doctor. The location shoot didn't merely showcase the return of River Song, though, as the beach had been used on *Doctor Who* previously as Bad Wolf Bay, the site of the touching parting between the Tenth Doctor and Rose.

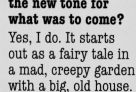

The thirty-first series of *Doctor Who* opened with a bang, as the Doctor's exploding TARDIS crashed into a young Amelia Pond's back garden. With the Doctor barely regenerated, he was thrust into a dangerous adventure revolving around a mysterious crack, Prisoner Zero and the misguided Atraxi, who threatened to incinerate Earth, all over a period of fourteen years!

The Eleventh Hour broke BBC iPlayer records, with over two million downloads of the episode. Critically, Matt, Karen and Steven Moffat were congratulated for heralding a new era in style!

Q&A

Episode one takes place in a quiet English village, a very classic series setting, do you think it was a good episode to showcase the new tone for what was to come?

Yes, I do. It starts out as a fairy tale in a mad, creepy garden with a big, old house.

How much pressure was there when you were filming the first episode?

Quite a lot. I rang my dad every night that first week in panic. But you have to battle on and be brave and that's what I tried to do.

You didn't film episode one first – was that to give you time to introduce a Doctor that you'd got used to?

Partly yes, which was a wise move, from clever old Piers Wenger. But I think it was also partly due to the locations as well.

THE EXECS

Although Steven Moffat is the lead writer and showrunner on the latest incarnation of *Doctor Who*, he doesn't run it alone. A pair of executive producers in the form of Beth Willis and Piers Wenger (who is also Head of Drama from BBC Wales) approve every aspect of the new show as it's in production, as well as making sure it comes in on time!

CAITLIN BLACKWOOD

The young Amelia Pond was played by Caitlin Blackwood, Karen Gillan's real-life cousin! Although the two had never met, Karen asked the producers to consider her and they brought Caitlin in to audition. The family resemblance was striking and she impressed, despite not having any acting training! Karen and Caitlin met for the first time on the set of *The Eleventh Hour*, but it wasn't until *The Big Bang* that they appeared on-screen together.

THE WHONIVERSE

The Doctor's universe is vast and complicated and over the course of all his time travelling escapades his past timelines don't always match up with the present. There are, however, a few constants in the 'Whoniverse' that tend to crop up throughout his adventures.

The Doctor's relationship with the Royal Family has been a rocky one, but whilst his encounters with both Queen Elizabeth I and Queen Victoria have been rocky at best, his reputation for saving the planet seems to have smoothed things over by the time of Queen Elizabeth II. In fact, by the time he meets Liz Ten, he's positively a legend!

Queen Victoria

Solar flares have been a problem for planet Earth throughout the Doctor's life, and not only was it roasted some time before the 29th Century, causing the construction of *Starship UK*, but again during the 30th Century. There the Fourth Doctor discovered humanity orbiting the planet in hibernation, waiting for it to become habitable once again.

The girl who waited's wait is over, as the Doctor whisks her off to the far future, and the UK, rebuilt amongst the stars. But *Starship UK* holds a dark secret and behind the smiling enforcers of the Police State is a truth every citizen wants to forget. It's up to the Doctor, Amy and Liz Ten to get to the bottom of the ship and unravel the mystery of the last Star Whale.

Q&A

Episode two was your first foray into a truly futuristic adventure. How hard is it to take that leap into a completely different world?

Easy! It's loads of fun, like playing – which is what acting is in many respects. The worlds and sets of *Doctor Who* are like magic acting material. They do so much of the imagining for you. It's bliss, I tell you, bliss.

THE NEW DALEKS!

The Daleks are the Doctor's oldest and deadliest foes and the Time Lord has fought them in more than twenty on-screen adventures! Created by the scientist Davros, the creatures were genetically mutated to feel nothing but hate and to exterminate all life that was not their own. Over the years the Doctor has attempted to avert or alter their creation, but to no avail and eventually the Daleks became so powerful that they went to war with the Time Lords themselves. Nothing but a handful of survivors escaped the war on either side and now the scavengers have been reborn with pure Dalek DNA, bigger, brighter and more deadly than ever. Their intimidating height and specialised ranks make them a truly formidable force and it's only a matter of time before they amass an army powerful enough to take on the galaxy once more.

The Supreme – leader of the Daleks.

WHITE

The Eternal – a mysterious member of the Dalek elite, the Eternal is never far from the Supreme's side.

YELLOW

The Scientist – responsible for research into the advancement and augmentation of Dalek technology.

ORANGE

The Strategist – acting as squad leaders, the strategists are capable of a wider perspective on any conflict than the lowly drones.

BLUE

The Drone – these foot soldiers of the new Dalek army make up the bulk of the ranks.

RED

Q & A

What's it like coming face to face with iconic monsters like the Daleks?

An honour, a mad honour, which you can't quite compute. They're icons of design and culture really, and I'm the man who fends them off! It felt like a real moment.

Is it exciting to see new incarnations of old monsters, like the new Daleks?

It's always good to see old monsters coming back. They're so popular because they're still here – you can't kill them off, they're too strong – so we have to like them!

Answering a call for help from Prime Minister Winston Churchill, the Doctor arrives in the darkest days of the London Blitz to discover that the Allies' new allies are the Daleks! When the Doctor finally exposes the evil creatures for what they are he realises that he has accidentally triggered the birth of a new Dalek race – but with Earth under threat from a living bomb, does he have time to get rid of his ancient enemies once and for all?

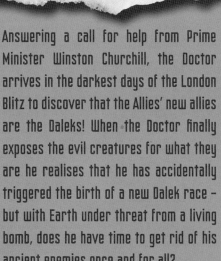

River Song summons the Doctor to the crash of the *Byzantium* where she is trying to earn her freedom by aiding a group of Clerics in the destruction of a Weeping Angel. Hunting it through the catacombs below the wreckage of the ship, the Doctor is shocked to discover an entire army of Angels that have lain dormant for millennia, and now they're waking up. As Amy succumbs to an Angel in her mind, the Doctor and River's only hope of escape is the crack from Amy's bedroom and a sense of gravity...

THE WEEPING ANGELS

Filming the Weeping Angels is a tricky task, as the creatures are in fact all played by actresses rather than static models. After attaching masks, wings and stone-like clothing to their bodies and heads, the actresses' skin is then painted with a similar stone effect. During the shooting of a scene the masks need to be swapped between shots. The inevitable wobble caused by requiring a person to stand motionless for so long is removed using digital techniques, a procedure that was considerably more tricky to perform than in *Blink*, due to the large numbers of Angels and the fact that other, moving characters are often in the same shot.

RIVER SONG

Played by former *ER* star Alex Kingston, River Song has a special relationship with the Doctor and is in possession of his most intimate secrets, including his name. It appears so far that the two have been encountering each other in reverse up until now, with the Tenth Doctor bearing witness to her death and her subsequent appearance in *The Pandorica Opens* taking place before *The Time of Angels*. Luckily, River has her own diary of her travels with the Doctor so that she can keep track of when she is encountering him in his life. There's nothing worse than accidentally giving away a spoiler...

Q&A

What's it like meeting characters like River Song, who has met the Doctor before but not your Doctor? Is it strange having to act familiar with someone that you have never met before in real life?

I suppose, but it's acting and you have to pretend, so no! I love River, what a character! She has intimate knowledge of the Doctor, which not many people do. It's maddening for him.

Was it cool to face the Weeping Angels for the first episode you filmed and did facing a returning enemy make it easier to settle into the role?

They're my favourite enemy, so yes, it was cool, but definitely not easier! The Angels were a nightmare to film with, as there was lots of technical stuff and prosthetics to deal with.

In the Weeping Angels two-parter, you had to play two distinctly different Doctors. How did you approach playing a 'future Doctor' so early in the run?

I only had one scene to go on and Steven Moffat wanted the back story of it to remain a surprise for me. He didn't want me to know too much about the "future" storyline, so I looked at my half a page of the script to work out what was going on and tried to tell the truth.

THE DRUNK GIRAFFE

On set, Matt is infamous for breaking things, to such an extent that showrunner Steven Moffat has nicknamed him the "drunk giraffe". Apparently he has managed to break several sonic screwdriver props as well as various controls from the TARDIS console! During filming of *The Time of Angels*, Matt managed to rip a handrail from the ceiling of River Song's Shuttle HQ, but the rest of the crew thought it so funny that they actually repeated the accident again for the finished take.

Q&A

Do foreign shoots make an episode feel more special to you?

We get to go on holiday! Yes, the visual feel is great. It succeeds in transporting us without computer graphics, which is great, and it gives things a feeling of ambition.

How do you think the introduction of Rory changed the TARDIS dynamic?

It was great. I love acting with Arthur and I think, comically, him and the Doctor have some interesting stuff together.

How does the Doctor affect Rory and Amy's relationship?

He gets in the way!

The Doctor's plans to take Rory and Amy to Venice for a romantic date back-fire, when they arrive to find the city quarantined and controlled by the sinister Rosanna Calvierri – an alien mother who plans to transform the young women of Venice into man-eating alien fish, before sinking the city in the greatest storm the world has ever seen.

ARTHUR DARViLL

Amy's long-suffering boyfriend is played by actor, musician and composer Arthur Darvill. The same age as Matt, Arthur and the future Doctor first met whilst in a stage adaptation of the film *Swimming with Sharks*. After receiving critical acclaim performing in a variety of plays, Arthur made the move to television in 2008, starring in *Little Dorrit*, a series based on the popular book by Charles Dickens. Recently, as well as defending Amy for 2000 years as the lone centurion, he also managed to feature briefly in the latest *Robin Hood* movie!

Although Matt is always keen to do his own stunts during filming, a stuntman is often called in to perform some of the more dangerous moves. During a take Matt will provide a jumping-off point, where he will be pulled backwards or fall onto a crash mat. The camera will then cut to a shot of the stuntman throwing himself backwards (either using a trampoline or wires) before cutting back to Matt on the floor to finish the stunt. Despite this, during *Vampires in Venice*, Matt was keen to perform the dive away from the exploding house himself, and only had one take in which to do so due to the time-consuming placement of the explosives. A brave decision, considering that he had burnt his hand on an exploding sonic screwdriver only a few weeks before!

HEADING FOR A FALL

The Dream Lord is your dark side. What are the important elements that make up your character?

I think one of the most important elements is the blood on his hands – "one day he would just drop out of the sky and tear down your world". This man has a lot on his mind, a lot that is dark, which is why he looks at the world with such lightness and joy, he has to otherwise... well I dread to think!

With the TARDIS hijacked by the sinister Dream Lord, the TARDIS crew find themselves shifting between two alternate realities. The first is set five years into Amy and Rory's future, when the village of Upper Leadworth is invaded by Eknodines. The second is the TARDIS, present day, on a collision course with a frozen star. As time runs out, the Doctor, Amy and Rory must decide which reality, if any, is real.

Toby Jones

The sinister Dream Lord is a parody of everything the Doctor stands for and is played to creepy perfection by actor Toby Jones. Born in 1967, Toby started acting in the early 1990s and has appeared in more than twenty films, including voicing the character of Dobby the house elf in the Harry Potter films!

LEADWORTH

The boring town of Leadworth is, in fact, a real place. Situated north-west of Cardiff city centre, it is only a short distance from BBC Wales and sports its very own cathedral. For the filming of episode one, the village green was slightly redressed with shops, phone boxes and even a pond created to match the scripts! But not every Leadworth scene is filmed in the same place, and both Amy's house (and her aunt's), the ruined castle and the butcher are located further afield.

THE SILURIANS RETURN

Misnamed the "Silurians", this race of Homo Reptilia ruled Earth long before the human race had evolved beyond apes. But when their astronomers sighted a large body of rock on a collision course with the planet, they retreated under the surface to survive. The body of rock became the moon and the various tribes remained in hibernation whilst the humans inherited the surface above.

The Third Doctor first encountered the Silurians during his exile on Earth when the activity of a subterranean nuclear research centre revived a nearby tribe. These Silurians sported a third eye, which was capable of transmitting a powerful heat ray for use as a weapon. When the Doctor failed to negotiate with the tribe, UNIT destroyed the hibernation chambers, much to the Time Lord's dismay.

It was only a short while later that the Doctor encountered an aquatic tribe of creatures (described as "Sea Devils" by the sailors that saw them), but again any hope of peace was destroyed when a rival Time Lord, the Master, attempted to hijack the tribe for his own ends.

The Fifth Doctor has also encountered both the Silurians and Sea Devils in the far future. Working together, the two tribes attempted to use humanity's own nuclear weapons to ignite a war that would destroy the human race and leave the planet open for them to return.

Q & A

The death of a regular character, such as Rory, is a rare event. Do you find scenes like that harder to shoot because of the extra pressure?

No, I think its great to kill off big characters – American drama is not afraid to do it, and in the world of *Doctor Who* you can bring the dead back!

ELDANE

The amiable Silurian Elder and leader of the tribe, Eldane was woken from his cryogenic sleep by Malokeh in an attempt to reason with Restac before she declared war on the humans.

RESTAC

The aggressive military commander, Restac was revived when the human drilling threatened to destroy their city. Eager to overthrow the "apes" control of the planet, she attempted to revive her army but died when Eldane activated the toxic fumigation procedures.

ALAYA

Restac's sister, she was sent to the surface to investigate the cause of the drilling, but was captured by the humans in the village above. They accidentally killed her when she refused to reveal the antidote to the venom in her tongue.

When a drilling operation uncovers a subterranean Silurian city, the Doctor leaps at the opportunity to broker a peace between the two races. But with both species claiming ownership of the planet, the situation begins to deteriorate. As the Silurian military commander reawakens her troops from hibernation, the Doctor's last chance relies on the humans above to be the very best of humanity...

MALOKEH

The Silurian doctor, Malokeh and his descendants had remained awake whilst the others slept so that they could analyse the evolution of the planet above.

During a trip to the Musee D'Orsay, the Doctor and Amy stumble across an alien menace in one of Vincent van Gogh's paintings, and embark on a terrifying adventure with the unappreciated painter, battling not only extraterrestrial monsters, but Vincent's own.

Albert Einstein

A MEETING OF MINDS

During the six month wait between being cast as the Eleventh Doctor and the beginning of filming, Matt found inspiration in the guise of a real life genius – Albert Einstein. Using the iconic photo of the famous scientist sticking his tongue out, he began writing short stories based around his Doctor meeting Einstein, to work out how they would bounce off each other. He imagined that the Time Lord might become rather frustrated with the man's absent-mindedness. Matt also thought that a story involving both the Eleventh Doctor and Sherlock Holmes would be a fascinating meeting between two British icons, which occurred to him whilst Steven Moffat's other series, *Sherlock*, was being filmed in Cardiff simultaneously. Personally though, if Matt had his own TARDIS, he would rather visit the lost city of Atlantis or hang out with Frank Sinatra.

Richard Curtis, who scripted *Vincent and the Doctor*, is one of England's best known writers. His first big hit was with the TV series *Blackadder* in 1983 and he followed that up with both *Mr Bean* in 1990 and *The Vicar of Dibley* in 1994.

By the mid nineties he had already begun moving into films with hits such as *Four Weddings and a Funeral* and *Bridget Jones' Diary*. In 1985 he also co-founded the charity fundraiser Comic Relief, which is held once every two years.

Richard Curtis, amongst many others, is obviously a hugely established and popular writer. What's it like being on a show that can bring such big names in the world of film and television together? Are there any other writers that you wish would write an episode for you?

It's incredible to have people like Richard involved, it's a testament to the show really – it can attract the best. And it's a testament to the form of the show as well: infinite stories told in so many different ways. I'd love David Lynch to write one!

Due to the disjointed nature of filming *Doctor Who*, is it hard, especially in the particularly emotional episodes, to make sure your character is in the right frame of mind for each scene?

That's part of film-making really, everything is out of sync. So much of acting is about thinking only about the present, so all you can do is think about what's in front of you and play it with truth – and a bit of style.

A BARREL OF LAUGHS

James Cordon isn't the only comedian to have starred in *Doctor Who*; the Tenth Doctor's former companion Donna was played by Catherine Tate, the writer and star of *The Catherine Tate Show*, whilst stand-up comedian and creator of sitcoms such as *Phoenix Nights*, Peter Kay, played the Abzorbaloff in the episode *Love and Monsters*. Simon Pegg appeared in *The Long Game* and his *Spaced* co-star Jessica Hynes fell in love with the human Doctor in *Human Nature* and *The Family of Blood*. Finally, *Doctor Who* episode writer and member of *The League of Gentlemen*, Mark Gatiss, has also appeared as the main character in *The Lazarus Experiment*.

JAMES CORDEN

The Lodger isn't the only time that writer, actor and comedian James Corden's career has crossed with Matt Smith's; both of them appeared in the popular Alan Bennett play *The History Boys* during 2004 and 2005. Since then James has gone on to co-create the popular comedy shows *Gavin and Stacey* and *Horne and Corden* as well as writing and starring in his own movie!

Mysterious goings-on in a first floor flat on Aickman Road cause the Doctor to become Craig Owen's new flatmate. With Amy trapped in the TARDIS he must find a solution to the time experiments being performed upstairs whilst helping Craig's unrequited love Sophie to realise what's really keeping her in her call-centre career.

The Lodger is sort of a 'Doctor Who does a sitcom' episode. Do you agree that the format of the show is infinitely variable or are there some limitations to what makes an exciting Doctor Who story?

For Doctor Who to work, the Doctor has to be written well, since he drives so much of the narrative. But the show's form is so good that it can withstand most stories, I think, so long as a ghastly alien creature turns up!

As a big football man yourself, do you think Gareth Roberts wrote the match scenes especially for you?

I hope Gareth did write them for me, I really do!

The Lodger is an "Amy-lite" story. How do you feel the dynamic changes when the Doctor doesn't have a companion to back him up?

What happens is that he finds other companions, like James Corden!

In this episode we have the Doctor trying (and failing) to be a normal bloke. Is it hard to be alien in such a "normal" setting?

No, that's the bliss, and that's the humour – this alien drinking milk amongst other mundane activities. How wonderful was it to hear the Doctor in the shower? It's great to see him be "normal", because he really isn't!

Q&A

You described *Doctor Who* as a "fairy tale" and episode twelve is probably the most fairy tale-like. Why do you think fairy tales and *Doctor Who* are a good fit?

It's the magic and the myth and the timeless stories. The Doctor has many of the same qualities as fairy tales. *Doctor Who* can be anything, its form is so strong. I think the magic and wonder of space fits into the notion of fairy tale, especially with a bow tie-wearing alien at the centre!

Did you know about the crack and what would happen right from the start, or did Steven keep those secret until later?

No! It was so secret! Only he knew and he is all-knowing!

Obviously throughout the last episode you need to keep track of which version of the Doctor you are, and when. Is it a struggle in both practical and 'acting' terms to keep the Doctor's behaviour (and costume) consistent?

In costume terms it was, because it involved several changes. In acting terms, no: you pretend and acting is about change.

Have you been told about the Silence and River Song's secret yet, or is that a secret even to you?!

Again, it's too much of a secret!

As the cracks in the universe continue to spread, Vincent van Gogh receives a vision of the TARDIS exploding. The trail of clues finally lead the Doctor and Amy to Stonehenge, where they are reunited with River Song to discover that the mythical Pandorica is in fact a reality. But when a resurrected Rory arrives as a Roman soldier, the Doctor realises too late that the whole scenario is a trap concocted by an alliance of his deadliest enemies. They imprison him in an attempt to halt the destruction of the universe – just as the TARDIS explodes with River Song trapped inside. As the universe ceases to have ever existed, the Doctor must use all his time travel skills to reboot existence, but his own survival depends on the memories of his companion, Amy...

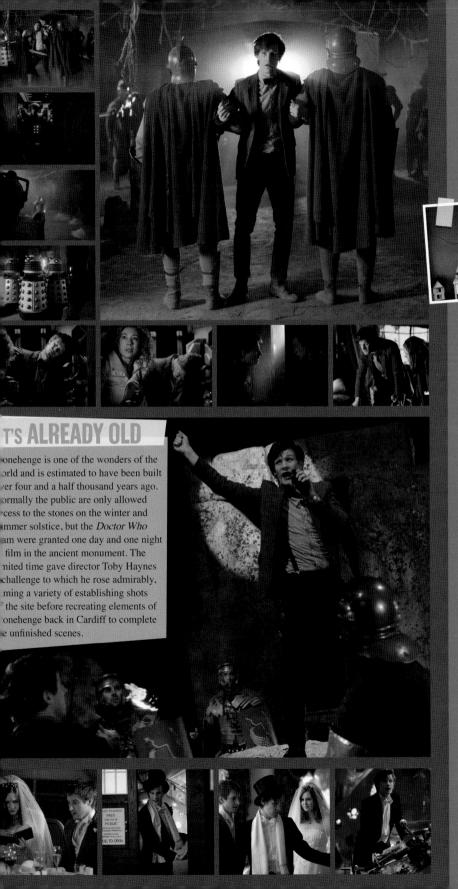

DID YOU SPOT THEM ALL?

With the cracks finally closed, did you spot them all?

THE ELEVENTH HOUR:

In Amy's wall and on the TARDIS scanner wave-form.

THE BEAST BELOW: In the side of *Starship UK*.

VICTORY OF THE DALEKS: Behind the TARDIS in the war cabinet.

FLESH AND STONE: In the wall of the flight deck.

VAMPIRES IN VENICE: The Saturnynes escaped through the crack to Venice as their home-world died.

COLD BLOOD: In the wall of the cave.

THE LODGER: In the wall of Craig's kitchen.

THE PANDORICA OPENS: In the TARDIS scanner.

THE BIG BANG: On the TARDIS main view-screen and a flashback to the road outside Craig's flat.

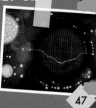

IT'S ALREADY OLD

Stonehenge is one of the wonders of the world and is estimated to have been built over four and a half thousand years ago. Normally the public are only allowed access to the stones on the winter and summer solstice, but the *Doctor Who* team were granted one day and one night to film in the ancient monument. The limited time gave director Toby Haynes a challenge to which he rose admirably, filming a variety of establishing shots of the site before recreating elements of Stonehenge back in Cardiff to complete the unfinished scenes.

BEFORE WHO

At twenty-seven, Matt's still in the early stages of his career, but his route to becoming the Doctor has been far from straightforward. Before he considered acting as a profession, Matt's goals and ambitions whilst at Northampton School for Boys could have taken him in a very different direction until an accident changed his life dramatically.

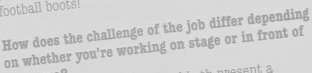

Q & A

What were your ambitions whilst at school?
I wanted to be a footballer and only a footballer. I lived it – I even used to go to sleep in my new football boots!

How does the challenge of the job differ depending on whether you're working on stage or in front of a camera?
Both forms require truth, and both present a different set of challenges. On camera you can play a little more with unspoken emotions, because a close-up will reveal every moment. But in truth I'm still working it out. I've improved a lot as a result of playing the Doctor, for sure – just from being in every scene, every day.

One of the real challenges is turnaround time. On stage you would have a four-week preparation period; on camera there isn't really any, and the line learning is often done the night before. But I like that about film – how instantaneous it is, capturing moments and keeping them forever.

Which do you prefer?
Whichever one I'm not doing!

TREADING THE BOARDS

Matt's involvement in the National Youth Theatre during his time at university gave him not only his first theatre roles but also an agent, who managed to get him his first professional parts before he had even graduated. Over the next three years he performed to rave reviews in plays *The History Boys* and *Murder in the Cathedral*, before gaining his first television role in an adaptation of Philip Pullman's book, *The Ruby in the Smoke*.

A CHANGE OF GOALS

Whilst at Northampton School for Boys, Matt Smith began to realise his lifelong ambition to become a professional footballer. He played for the youth teams of Northampton, Nottingham Forest and Leicester Football Clubs. But after he suffered a serious back injury, his career was brought to an abrupt halt, as doctors advised him against further training for fear of causing worse problems down the line. Matt was devastated.

It was his drama teacher that managed to inspire Matt once again, signing him up to perform a small role in the school play and encouraging him to join the National Youth Theatre. Although initially reluctant, Matt soon discovered that he had a passion for acting, and once he left school he chose to study drama and creative writing at the University of East Anglia.

EARLY CAREER

After a successful and critically lauded series of performances in the theatre, Matt's first television role was in the first of two adaptations of the acclaimed author Philip Pullman's Sally Lockhart series of novels. With the main character played by former *Doctor Who* companion Billie Piper, both *The Ruby in the Smoke* and *The Shadow in the North* (made the following year) featured Matt Smith as the character Jim Taylor, a cockney lad who befriends Sally during her investigations into her father's death.

Q&A

Your first roles were in the Philip Pullman adaptations. Had you been a fan of Philip Pullman?
I'd never read a word, but of course I fell in love with his work.

What was the character of Jim Taylor like to play? You Met *Doctor Who* companion Billie Piper there as well...
Great fun. Billie Piper was just a joy, so kind and so giving. It was my first job on screen and I was a bit nervous, but Billie Piper was just a really good mate, and I loved making that show, I really did. Jim was sort of the artful dodger, so he was bliss to play.

Was it exciting being on TV for the first time? How did you celebrate?
When I found out I got that job, it was summer and I was living in Marylebone in London. I was so excited. I ran around a bit and called my dad!

51

The Future

Who are your inspirations?

My dad, Lindsay Duncan, Steven Moffat, Piers Wenger, Beth Willis, Eric Cantona, Zinedine Zidane, Stuart Pearce. I could meet a guy on the tube who reads his paper a certain way and that may inspire something new. As an actor, everyone is a bit of inspiration, but my dad has had the most profound influence on my life, for sure.

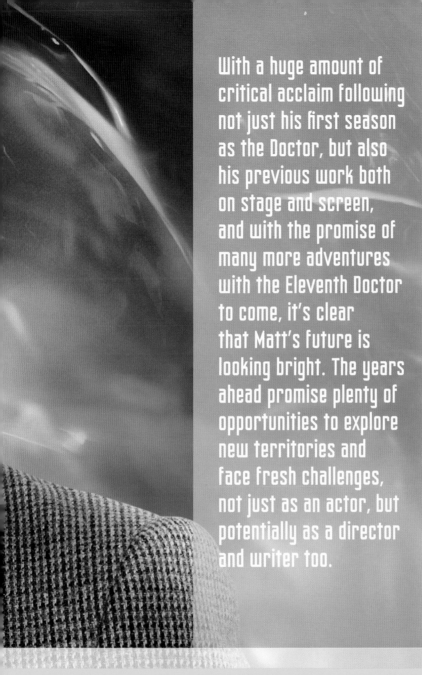

With a huge amount of critical acclaim following not just his first season as the Doctor, but also his previous work both on stage and screen, and with the promise of many more adventures with the Eleventh Doctor to come, it's clear that Matt's future is looking bright. The years ahead promise plenty of opportunities to explore new territories and face fresh challenges, not just as an actor, but potentially as a director and writer too.

Who would you like to work with?
Paddy Considine, Daniel Day Lewis, Shane Meadows, Andrea Arnold, and David Lynch – now that would be cool...

What type of an actor do you aspire to be?
A brilliant and truthful one, I guess. Someone that challenges the script and asks the right questions. I hope I remain instinctual, and I hope I set a good work ethic, as it were. When you play the Doctor it's important to drive things forward on set – make sure you know your lines the best!

Q & A

What films, television shows or plays have you always dreamed of being in?
I'd love to play Macbeth... and Batman! To be honest at the moment I really want to play a baddie – someone really mean. As a kid I just watched ninja movies so I'd always wanted to do one of them, and I'd love to play a musician – a doomed and dark musician!

Who do you think taught you the most?
Again my dad really, in terms of life and outlook, but as an actor Lindsay Duncan has been the greatest influence; she taught me so much about courage and consistency. I did a play with her called *That Face,* and to see her every night was a privilege and one from which I learnt so much. Music is always a great liberator of my imagination as well – it transports me and ignites my inventiveness, I think; Radiohead, Arcade Fire, Beethoven, Pink Floyd.

You're a keen musician as well. Is that something you want to pursue?
Music is a hobby, one I love, but I'm not very good! I like the feeling of getting better though and it's a nice escape from line learning.

What does the future hold for Matt Smith?
I don't know! Hopefully

challenging work and lots more *Doctor Who!* I want to keep stretching myself as an actor, going for parts that have danger and complexity.

Any specific ambitions?
I want to direct. I love taking photos and I'd love to work with actors; at the moment I'm working on some short films. I enjoy writing – short stories and things – so we'll see, who knows?

What do you think you'd be doing if you weren't an actor?
Who knows? I was going to study politics at Sheffield at one stage! Now I'd like to think I'd do something creative, that or become captain of Blackburn Rovers and a member of the England Team!

Would you prefer to stay in TV or the theatre, or would you like to move into films? You've talked about wanting to direct before...
Films are something I want to make, for sure. I love films, and to direct is definitely an ambition because I want more creative power!

FAST FACTS

NAME:
Matthew Robert Smith

DATE OF BIRTH:
28 October, 1982

EDUCATION:
Northampton School for Boys, the University of East Anglia, the National Youth Theatre

NICKAMES:
Smithers, Smithy

SPORTING ACHIEVEMENTS:
Played for Northampton Town, Nottingham Forest and Leicester City Youth Academy

MUSICAL ACHIEVEMENTS:
Played the drum in the school choir!

FAVOURITE THINGS TO DO ON A DAY OFF:
Play guitar and piano, watch football and eat out.

BAND: I love Radiohead

FOOD: Spaghetti Bolognese – a classic!

SONG: 'Weird Fishes', by Radiohead from the album, *In Rainbows*

BOOK: *The Master and Margarita* by Mikhail Bulgakov

FILM: *The Beat that my Heart Skipped*

SPORT TO PLAY: Football, of course! I used to play all the time before I was injured.

ANIMAL: A golden eagle or cats!

DOCTOR: Patrick Troughton

A Few of Matt's

TV SHOW: *Doctor Who*, of course! And I love *True Blood*.

PLACE TO GO: Rio is a fantastic city.

SPORT TO WATCH: Football. My favourite team is Blackburn Rovers!

COMPUTER GAME: Mario Cart... or European Soccer on the Sega Megadrive.

Favourite Things

THE MATT

Do you think you know all there is to know about Matt Smith? Can you remember all his fast facts and trivial trivia? Test your knowledge here with our quiz on the man behind the Eleventh Doctor! Remember, the answers are all in this book – somewhere!

1. What is Matt Smith's middle name?

   A. Robert
   B. James
   C. Adam

2. What date was the Eleventh Doctor's casting announced?

   A. 22 May 2009
   B. 3 January 2009
   C. 25 December 2009

3. In what play did both James Corden and Matt Smith star?

   A. *The Gruffalo*
   B. *Grease*
   C. *The History Boys*

4. What writer has both written an episode of *Doctor Who* for Matt Smith and starred in the show himself?

   A. Richard Curtis
   B. Steven Moffat
   C. Mark Gatiss

5. What musical instrument does Matt play?

   A. Drum
   B. Banjo
   C. Double bass

6. Which band have covered the *Doctor Who* theme tune?

   A. JLS
   B. Orbital
   C. Girls Aloud

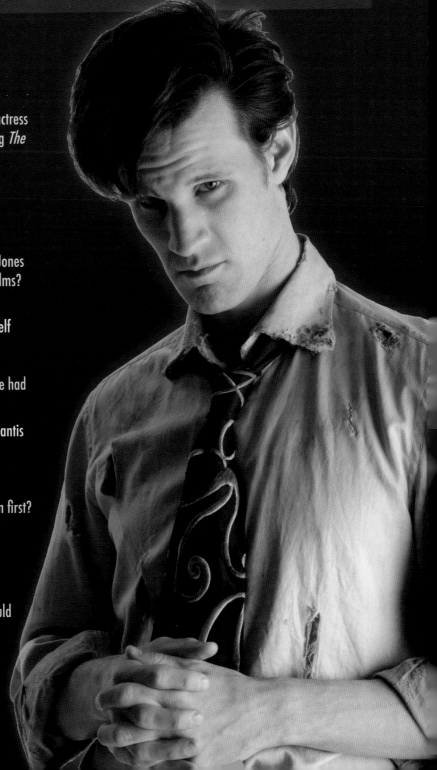

⌐ITH QUiZ!

former *Doctor Who* actress
tt meet whilst filming *The
the Smoke*?

   A. Billie Piper
   B. Catherine Tate
   C. Elisabeth Sladen

d Dream Lord Toby Jones
the *Harry Potter* films?

   A. Voldemort
   B. Dobby the house elf
   C. Tom Riddle

would Matt visit if he had
IS?

   A. The lost city of Atlantis
   B. The moon
   C. The future

episode did Matt film first?

   A. *The Big Bang*
   B. *Flesh and Stone*
   C. *The Beast Below*

ype of character would
ke to play next?

   A. A baddie
   B. A woman
   C. An alien

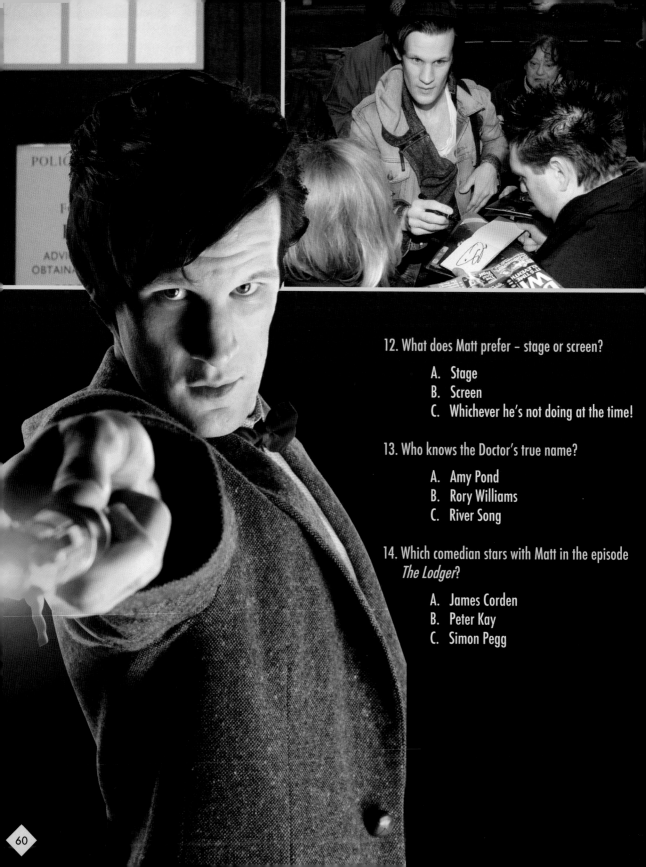

12. What does Matt prefer – stage or screen?

    A. Stage
    B. Screen
    C. Whichever he's not doing at the time!

13. Who knows the Doctor's true name?

    A. Amy Pond
    B. Rory Williams
    C. River Song

14. Which comedian stars with Matt in the episode *The Lodger*?

    A. James Corden
    B. Peter Kay
    C. Simon Pegg

15. Why did Matt get nicknamed "Doctor Who" whilst at university?

    A. He had a striped scarf
    B. He had a TARDIS
    C. He had a sonic screwdriver

16. How is young Amelia actress Caitlin Blackwood related to Karen Gillan?

    A. Sister
    B. Cousin
    C. She isn't

17. Who is Matt Smith's favourite Doctor?

    A. Patrick Troughton
    B. David Tennant
    C. William Hartnell

18. What Shakespeare character would Matt love to play?

    A. Macbeth
    B. Hamlet
    C. Othello

19. What was the name of Matt's secondary school?

    A. Abraham Guest Secondary
    B. Passmores School
    C. Northampton School for Boys

20. What's Matt Smith's favourite band?

    A. Radiohead
    B. Orbital
    C. Take That

ANSWERS: 1.A, 2.B, 3.C, 4.C, 5.A, 6.B, 7.A, 8.B, 9.A, 10.B, 11.A, 12.C, 13.C, 14.A, 15.A, 16.B, 17.A, 18.A, 19.C, 20.A

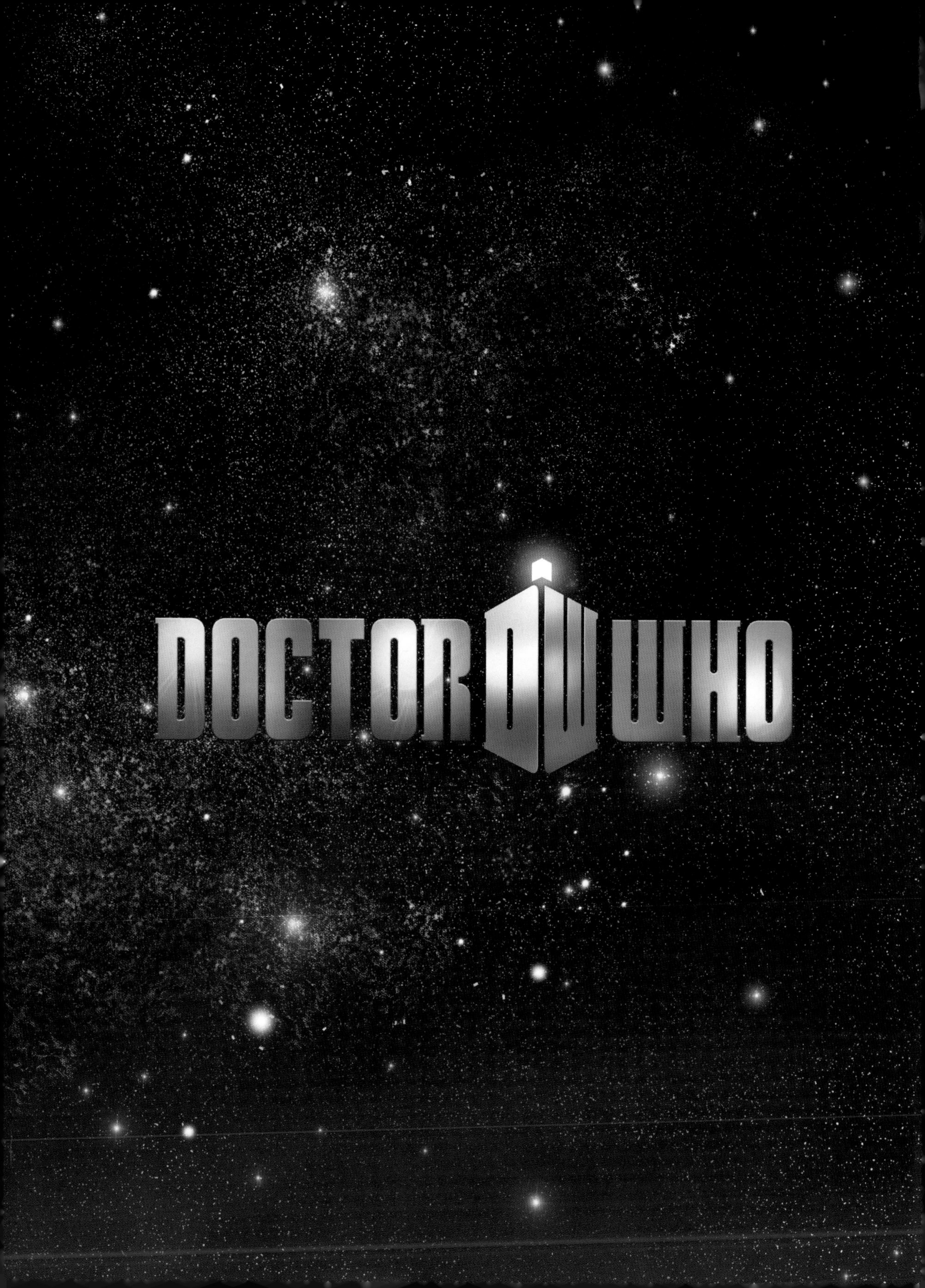
DOCTOR WHO